It's me...
a Dog

An imprint of Om Books International

First Published in 2019 by

Om KIDZ | Om Books International

Corporate & Editorial Office
A-12, Sector 64, Noida 201 301
Uttar Pradesh, India
Phone: +91 120 477 4100
Email: editorial@ombooks.com
Website: www.ombooksinternational.com

Sales Office
107, Ansari Road, Darya Ganj
New Delhi 110 002, India
Phone: +91 11 4000 9000
Email: sales@ombooks.com
Website: www.ombooks.com

© Om Books International 2019

ISBN: 978-93-86410-45-0

Printed in India

10 9 8 7 6 5 4 3 2 1

Contents

WHO ARE YOU?

Hello! I am a dog. I belong to the Canidae family and I am a subspecies of the gray wolf.

Scientific Name

Canis lupus familiaris

My babies are called puppies.

WHERE DO YOU LIVE?

I am a domestic mammal and humans love to keep me as a pet because I am a very friendly animal. I live in a kennel when in domesticity. Many of us are also found in the wild. We were one of the first animals to be domesticated.

HOW BIG ARE YOU?

We can be as huge as a Great Dane, which can be around 35 to 44 inches tall and as small as the Chihuahua, which is around 5 inches tall. There are over 400 breeds of dogs.

Great Dane

Chihuahua

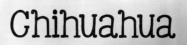

English Mastiff

World's Heaviest Dogs

English Mastiffs, which weigh over 105 kg, are the heaviest dogs in the world.

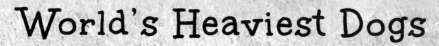

WHAT DO YOU LIKE TO EAT?

We eat various kinds of food — red meat, vegetables, bread, grains, eggs, milk and so on.

Sharp Teeth

Dogs have 42 permanent teeth, while puppies have 28 teeth.

WHY ARE YOU KNOWN AS MAN'S BEST FRIEND?

We are known as 'man's best friend' because we are extremely loyal and protective. We have been companions to humans for over 12,000 years now.

Protectors and Companions

Dogs have been around humans as protectors and hunting companions.

CAN YOU SENSE HUMAN EMOTIONS?

Yes. We can read the facial expressions of humans, show our empathy and also display jealousy. We learn all this by observing humans.

WHAT ARE YOUR BEST TRAITS?

I am alert, curious, intelligent, fearless, playful, friendly, **affectionate**, loyal, **agile** and have a strong sense of smell.

New words to learn

Agile - Move quickly and easily
Affectionate - Show fondness

DO YOU HAVE A STRONG SENSE OF SMELL?

Yes. We are famous for our strong sense of smell. It is several times stronger than that of humans. This is why the police department has sniffer dogs, which help them detect bombs and nab culprits.

Unique Noseprints

Just like humans have unique fingerprints, dogs have unique noseprints, which can be used to identify them.

CAN YOU SEE IN THE DARK?

Yes! We have a special membrane in our eyes, which helps us to see in the dark. We have three eyelids – an upper lid, a lower lid and a third lid, which is known as haw or a nictitating membrane. The haw helps to keep our eyes moist and protected.

Not Colour Blind

We are not colour blind. We can see some colours. We can differentiate between blue and yellow, but not between red and green.

HOW DO YOU MAINTAIN YOUR BODY TEMPERATURE?

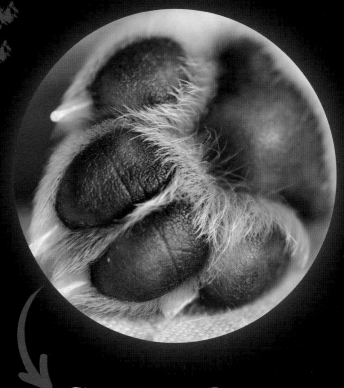

Our fur helps us in keeping warm. We cool ourselves down by panting.

Smelly Paws

Our sweat glands are present in our paw pads. This is the reason why we have smelly paws.

CAN YOU LEARN TRICKS?

Yes. We are very intelligent and can be easily trained. Dog owners often teach their pets a variety of adorable tricks.

Smart Canines

Dogs are as smart as a 2-year-old child. Studies say that canines can pick up 165 words on an average. Some of the more intelligent dogs can learn up to 250 words.

Guide dogs, also known as 'seeing-eye' or 'service dogs', are dogs that are professionally trained to protect, help and guide their visually impaired owners.

Dogs are Used in Therapy

Dogs are used as a part of therapy in nursing homes and hospitals as they provide comfort and affection to patients and help them to recover fast.

15

CAN YOU DREAM?

Yes! Research proves that we can dream just like humans. We may twitch, growl, move our legs or quiver while dreaming.

WHY DO YOU CURL UP?

We have an age-old instinct to curl up to protect our vital organs from predators, and to keep ourselves warm.

Tail Wagging

It is assumed that we only wag our tails when we are happy and friendly, but that is not true. We also wag our tails to express strong emotions, such as anger.

CAN YOU TELL ME ABOUT BASENJIS?

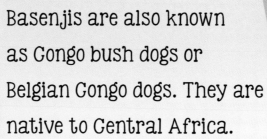

Basenjis are also known as Congo bush dogs or Belgian Congo dogs. They are native to Central Africa.

Basenji, a breed of hunting dog, is known as a barkless dog. While we cannot bark, we can make a variety of sounds which can be best described as yodelling.

Yes. Dalmatians are smart and friendly dogs. We are also known as English coach dogs, firehouse dogs and plum-pudding dogs.

Dalmatian Pups

When Dalmatian puppies are born, they are pure white. They develop black spots as they grow older.

19

WHO ARE SHIH TZUS?

Walk Time

These pint-sized pooches love to go for walks. They are affectionate, energetic and sweet-tempered.

Shih Tzu is a Tibetan breed of dogs. It is a long-haired, alert and active canine which is around 10 inches tall and weighs around 4 to 7 kg. The Shih Tzu has a dense coat, hanging ears and a short muzzle.

WHY DO YOU HAVE WHISKERS?

Our whiskers help us to pick up changes in the air currents. Whiskers help us to gauge important information about the shape, speed and size of nearby objects.

Grooming Time

A lot of time and effort is required to groom the Shih Tzu's long and shiny hair. You need to brush its coat several times a week.

A Dog with Six Toes

Norwegian Lundehund is the only breed of dog which has six toes on each paw.

ACTIVITY TIME

DALMATIAN PUPPET

Things You'll Need

- A paper lunch bag
- White paint
- Coloured paper
- Scissors
- Glue bottle
- Googly eyes

Paint the paper bag white and let it dry.

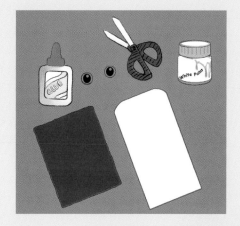

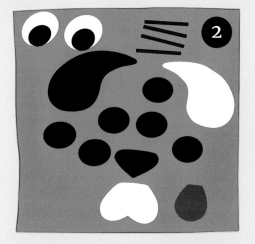

Cut out different parts of the face of the dog, from black, white and red paper.

Glue the upside down heart-shaped cutout onto the bag.

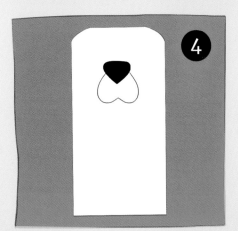

Glue the nose onto the paper bag.

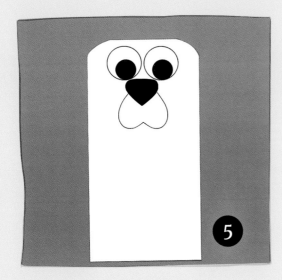

Glue the googly eyes above the nose.

Glue the ears onto the sides of the head. Glue the tongue underneath the flippy tab so you can see part of the circle sticking out from under the muzzle.

Glue two whiskers (long, thin rectangular strips) onto either side of the upside-down heart shape.

Glue as many spots as you like on the puppet. And voilà, your dog puppet is ready!

The puppy is hungry.
Help it reach the bone.